No Queen, Today!

Written by Jill Eggleton
Illustrated by Clive Taylor

The queen woke up one morning and she looked at her queen clothes. "I am not wearing those today," she said.

The maid began to flap and fluster. "You must," she said. "You are a queen!"

But the queen stamped her foot and said...

"I have been,
I have been,
I have been
a queen,
and it is
a terrible bore!

I have been,
I have been,
I have been
a queen,
and I won't be
one anymore!"

The queen went into
the palace kitchen.
"Eggs," she said.
"I will cook some eggs."

The cooks began
to flap and fluster.
**"You mustn't!
You mustn't!"**
they shouted.
"You are a queen!"

But the queen
stamped her foot
and said…

"I have been,
I have been,
I have been
a queen,
and it is
a terrible bore!

I have been,
I have been,
I have been
a queen,
and I won't be
one anymore!"

The queen went into the palace garden. "Weeds," she said. "I will pull out weeds."

The gardener began to flap and fluster. **"You mustn't! You mustn't!"** he shouted. **"You are a queen!"**

But the queen stamped her foot and said…

"I have been,
I have been,
I have been
a queen,
and it is
a terrible bore!

I have been,
I have been,
I have been
a queen,
and I won't be
one anymore!"

The queen saw a horse by the palace gates. "A horse," she said. "I will ride to town."

So off she went singing...

"I *have been*, I *have been*, I *have been* a queen, and I won't be one anymore!"

But...
when the queen
got to town, she heard
an horrendous noise.
People were
sitting in the street,
and they were weeping
and wailing...

"We have no queen.
We have no queen.
What a terrible,
terrible thing!
We have no queen.
We have no queen.
We will have to find
a king!"

King Wanted

Must be clever and kind

Call at palace.

"A king!"
screeched the queen.
"You can't have a king!"

She rushed back
to the palace
and put on
her queen clothes.

"Hurray!"
shouted the people.
"The queen is back.
We don't have to find
a king!"

But once every year,
the queen
will not wear
her queen clothes.

And the people
in the palace
hear her say…

"I won't be
a queen.
I won't be
a queen.
I won't be
a queen today!"

Guide Notes

Title: No Queen Today!
Stage: Year 3

Genre: Fiction
Approach: Shared Reading
Processes: Thinking Critically, Exploring Language, Processing Information
Written and Visual Focus: Change of text style and font, Poster

THINKING CRITICALLY
(sample questions)
- What do you think this story could be about?
- Why do you think the queen feels her job is boring?
- Why do you think the queen wanted to cook eggs and weed the garden?
- What do you think the people thought had happened to the queen?
- Why do you think the queen was upset about the people wanting a king?
- What sort of things do you think the queen will do on her day off?
- Do you think this story could be true? Why/Why not?

EXPLORING LANGUAGE

Terminology
Title, cover, illustrations, author, illustrator

Vocabulary
Interest words: flap, fluster, bore, horrendous, weeping, wailing, screeched, maid, palace
Contractions: don't, won't, mustn't
Compound words: anymore, today
Singular/Plurals: maid/maids, egg/eggs, weed/weeds, gate/gates, person/people
Antonyms: whispered/shouted, morning/night, queen/king
Homonyms: been/bean, one/won, heard/herd, wailing/whaling
Synonyms: horrendous/terrible/awful, flap/fluster, shouted/yelled

Print Conventions
Capital letter for sentence beginnings, title and heading (for poster), full stops, exclamation marks, quotation marks, commas, question marks, ellipses, apostrophes